Anonymous

Richfield Springs

Anonymous

Richfield Springs

ISBN/EAN: 9783337732271

Printed in Europe, USA, Canada, Australia, Japan

Cover: Foto ©ninafisch / pixelio.de

More available books at **www.hansebooks.com**

Richfield Springs,

OTSEGO CO., N. Y.,

AND

The New American.

PUBLISHED FOR

URIAH WELCH,

BY

DEMPSEY & CARROLL, ART STATIONERS,

Union Square, N. Y.

TO THE READER:

This little book has been prepared for the purpose of recalling more vividly to the minds of our former guests and patrons, recollections of the pleasant scenes and tranquil enjoyments of their previous visits, and by these happy reminiscences to remind them, and through them their friends, of the unusual opportunities afforded at Richfield Springs for the enjoyment of rest, recreation, refined pleasures and restored health.

The experience of many invalids has shown that the greatest benefit is derived by taking a course of baths early in the season, and returning after a sojourn at Saratoga, the mountains, or the sea-shore, to take a second course. Persons in delicate health following this plan may find a choice of rooms more easily obtainable, and avoid the excitement of the midsummer season.

The following analysis of the NEW SPRING was recently made under the supervision of Prof. F. LeRoy Satterlee, M.D., Ph. D., of New York City, who has devoted much time to the study of Rheumatism and allied disorders.

ANALYSIS OF SULPHUR SPRING.

Temperature 50° Fahrenheit.
One U. S. Gallon of 231 cubic inches contains :

	GRAINS.
Hydrosulphuric Acid, (free)	5,276
Sulphuric Acid in Sulphates :	
Calcium Sulphate, Magnesium Sulphate, Sodium Sulphate and Potassium Sulphate, ...	76,787
Sulphur in Sulphides :	
Calcium Sulphide, &c., .	4,366
Sulphur in Hyposulphites :	
Calcium Hyposulphite, &c.,	2,556
Chlorine in Chlorides :	
Sodium Chloride and Potassium Chloride,	1,572
Carbonic Acid in Carbonates :	
Calcium Carbonate and Magnesium Carbonate, .	9,264
Lime, ...	39,381
Magnesia, ...	13,763
Soda, ...	12,730
Potassa, ...	8,222
Silica, ...	0,911
Alumina, ...	0,104
Iron Oxide, ...	0,213
LITHIUM, ...	0,921
Strontium, ...	a trace
Barium, ...	a trace
Total Solids,	170,815

LOCATION ✦ OF ✦ RICHFIELD ✦ SPRINGS,

CONSPICUOUS AS A HEALTH RESORT.

DISTANCES AND POINTS OF COMPASS BY RAILWAY.

New York City to Richfield Springs, North West.	250 miles
Philadelphia	"	"	"	North, . . 300 "
Boston	"	"	West, . . . 300 "
Albany	"	"	"	" . . . . 100 "
Saratoga Springs "	"	"	"	100 "
Rochester	"	"	"	East, ... 150 "
Niagara Falls	"	"	"	"	200 "
Utica	"	"	"	South, . . . 30 "
Thousand Islands "	"	"	" . . . 140 "

— — —

THE NEW AMERICAN,

RICHFIELD SPRINGS, N. Y.,

URIAH WELCH, Owner and Proprietor,

Opens June 13th, Closes September 15th.

Communications at other times than above months should be sent to the
ST. NICHOLAS, NEW YORK CITY.

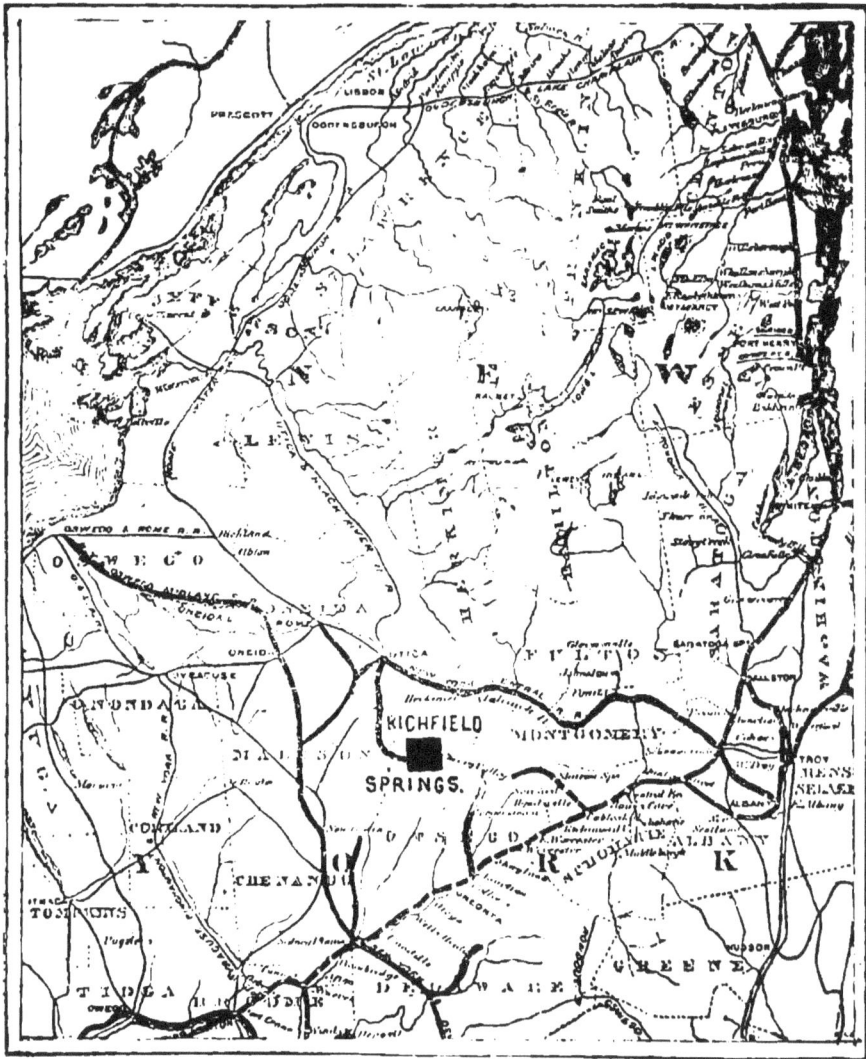

MAP OF NORTHERN AND CENTRAL NEW YORK.

Richfield Springs, N. Y.

Its Location and Attractions.

SULPHUR SPRING AND PARK.

There is not in the wide world a valley so sweet
As that vale, in whose bosom the bright waters meet;
Oh, the last rays of feeling and life must depart
Ere the bloom of that valley shall fade from my heart!
—THOMAS MOORE.

LOCALITY OF THE SPRINGS.

THE SPRINGS are situated in the north-easterly portion of the county of Otsego, bordering on the county of Herkimer, in the midst of a region unsurpassed in reputation for healthfulness and longevity, as well as for the natural beauty of its scenery. The village of Richfield is in its altitude not less than *twelve hundred feet above the valley of the historical Mohawk*, and distant about ten miles from it, while the valley of the Susquehanna, but little more remote, lies in the opposite direction. The Springs are situated upon the elevated region between the two. The landscape is variegated with undulating hills and vales and villages, while numerous lakes lie sleeping about, being the most beautiful in the Empire State.

Independent of the benefit to be derived from the mineral waters, no more desirable residence can be found for delicate persons during the Summer and Fall months. The air is invigorating. never oppressively hot, the thermometer ranging from 60° to 80° during the summer months, rendering exercise in the open air enjoyable, and devoid of fatigue at any hour of the day.

Its drainage and elevation are probably the source of its great salubrity, and it is the most healthful summer resort for those desiring a change from sea air, absolutely free from mosquitoes and malaria, and a safe retreat from hay fever.

The temperature is delightful, several degrees less than the river valleys or New York City the nights being always cool and refreshing. There is withal an unusual clearness in the atmosphere which enables the elevation to command views of landscape unsurpassed in beauty and grandeur. Behind every root and tree there is a hidden spirit peeping out, for it is with the neighborhood of this place that some of the most renowned of Cooper's fictions have incorporated themselves with the landscape. All these circumstances combine to give interest to the strolls, drives, and rides, the fishing and pleasure parties, which of late years are so popular at Richfield Springs.

Richfield is one of those rare centres toward which the cultivated and the intellectual naturally gravitate, for here they find, gathered as it were into a magnetic centre, whatever is essential to the highest pleasure of the senses, as well as of the mind. Its attractions are so genuine, so far beyond all that is false and meretricious, that no one experiences anything like satiety. Richfield grows upon one like a friend. There is a natural simplicity, an elegant repose, a breezy freshness about the spot which captivate the senses and fascinate the mind. Season after season you will meet the same faces, and this contributes to give a home-like aspect to the place.

> 'Twas that friends, the beloved of my bosom, were near,
> Who made every dear scene of enchantment more dear,
> And who felt how the best charms of Nature improve
> When we see them reflected from looks that we love.
>> —THOMAS MOORE.

FISHING.

Are you a disciple of Izaak Walton? Here streams and lakes abound. The still-water fishing is excellent, and trouting in the neighboring brooks offer great sport.

> " Princess of lakes, how I love
>   Upon thy flowery banks to lie,
> And view thy silver stream,
>   When gilded by a Summer's beam !
> And in it all thy wanton fry
>   Playing at liberty,
> And with my angle upon them
>   The all of treachery
> I ever learn'd industriously to try !"

HUNTING AND GAME.

Are you a hunter? The woods abound in woodcock, partridges, squirrels and other game.

HORSEBACK RIDING.

What a wild thought of triumph, that this girlish hand
Such a steed in the might of his strength may command !
What a glorious creature !   Ah ! glance at him now,
As I check him a while on this green hillock's brow;
How he tosses his mane, with a shrill joyous neigh,
And paws the firm earth in his proud, stately play !
Hurrah ! off again, dashing on as in ire,
Till the long, flinty pathway is flashing with fire !
Ho ! a ditch !—Shall we pause ?   No; the bold leap we dare,
Like a swift-wingèd arrow we rush through the air !
Oh, not all the pleasures that poets may praise,
Not the 'wildering waltz in the ball-room's blaze,
Nor the chivalrous joust, nor the daring race,
Nor the swift regatta, nor merry chase,
Nor the sail, high heaving waters o'er,
Nor the rural dance on the moonlight shore,
Can the wild and thrilling joy exceed
Of a fearless leap on a fiery steed !

—GRACE GREENWOOD.

ROMANTIC SWAINS AND DAMES.

"Are you a lover, or melancholy swain, seeking for 'some one to love?' Then Richfield, with its wild woods and its coteries of pretty maids, is the very spot for thee."

BALCONY OF NEW AMERICAN.

" How calm and quiet a delight
    Is it, alone
To read, and meditate. and write,
    By none offended, and offending none !
To walk, ride, sit, or sleep at one's own ease:
And, pleasing one's self, none other to displease."

THE NEW AMERICAN.

RICHFIELD SPRINGS, N. Y.

THE LOCATION of *The New American* is the finest at the Springs and is especially convenient to the baths. Large airy rooms, open fire places, steam heat in the halls and public rooms, with every comfort for *those accustomed to the best society* and first-class accommodations. The supplies are the best that the market affords and are daily received from New York City, being selected by the steward of my New York hotel, "*The St. Nicholas.*" *The New American*, newly fitted and made complete in every desirable appointment, is not excelled, in these particulars, by any hotel in this country. We quote as applicable a

STANZA FROM "THE CASTLE OF INDOLENCE."

A pleasing land of drowsy-head it was,
  Of dreams that wave before the half-shut eye;
And of gay castles in the clouds that pass,
  Forever flashing round a summer sky!
There eke the soft delights, that witchingly
  Instill a wanton sweetness through the breast,
And the calm pleasures, always hovered nigh;
  But whate'er smacked of noyance or unrest,
Was far, far off expelled from this delicious nest.

LETTER from the Rev. Dr. Ormiston, of the Fifth Avenue Dutch Reformed Church, New York:

Seldom, if ever, have I enjoyed so delightful a holiday as the ten days I spent last Summer at RICHFIELD SPRINGS. The place is as remarkable for the great variety and rare beauty of the surrounding scenery as for the refreshing coolness and invigorating salubrity of the pure atmosphere.

This charming rural village is situated about 1,700 feet above the level of the sea, in the midst of a number of wood-crowned hills, whose sides, and the valleys lying between, are under good cultivation. A number of lovely lakes, fed by streamlets from the hills, lie in quiet beauty in the immediate neighborhood, easy of access to all who enjoy the exhilaration of an early morning walk, or the soothing influence of an evening ramble. Lake Canadarago, invested with the charm of many an Indian legend, and enchanting as an English lake or Scottish loch, is within one mile of the village, and furnishes every facility for rowing and fishing.

Otsego Lake, a gem of crystal clearness, rendered classic by the home, the pen, and the grave of Cooper, is within six miles. Its variegated shores, historic reminiscences, Indian tales, and literary associations all combine to make it an object of intense and memorable interest to all visitors.

Good country roads lead in every direction, over hill and dale, through wood and glen, by rippling brook and dashing cascade, past home-like farm houses and venerable mansions of ante-revolutionary record, so that an agreeable variety of drives may be daily enjoyed.

The Springs, which give the name and partially the celebrity to the place, are regarded as specially beneficial to all suffering from rheumatism and diseases of the blood.

The New American, recently purchased by Mr. U. Welch, of the St. Nicholas, New York, and refitted and refurnished at great expense, is second to no hotel in the country in its appointments and arrangements for the comfort and convenience of guests. The fact that The New American is under the personal superintendence of "mine host" of the St. Nicholas, is a sufficient guarantee that all which prolonged experience, abundant resources, and courtly attention can furnish will there be found.

As a place for the invalid or the wearied, seeking health and recreating rest, Richfield Springs presents strong attractions, and The New American opens for them a door to a home. I hope I may, at some future day, have the privilege of revisiting that scene of healthful, life-inspiring enjoyment.

W. ORMISTON.

NEW YORK, Jan., 1882.

Extract from a letter from F. H. Boynton, M. D., of 22 West 38th Street:

During my visit to RICHFIELD SPRINGS last Summer, I was much impressed with the beauty of its location and surroundings. The yearly increase in number of visitors, gives evidence of its growing popularity as a Summer resort. Its many pleasant drives and picturesque scenery, and lakes, affording opportunity for boating and excellent fishing, render it an attraction to pleasure seekers. Its Springs (Sulphur, Magnesia and Iron) have been found very beneficial in rheumatic and skin affections. Its freedom from malarial diseases and hay fever, makes it a desirable place of residence for those suffering from these complaints.

While there I observed the good effect of these waters upon cases of acute and chronic inflammatory, fibrous and muscular rheumatism, gout, and skin diseases in a marked degree.

Having derived decided benefit in my own case—fibrous rheumatism—from the use of the waters, it is my intention to spend my vacation there next summer.

READ REFERENCES ON PAGES 34, 35, 36 & 37.

THE NEW AMERICAN.

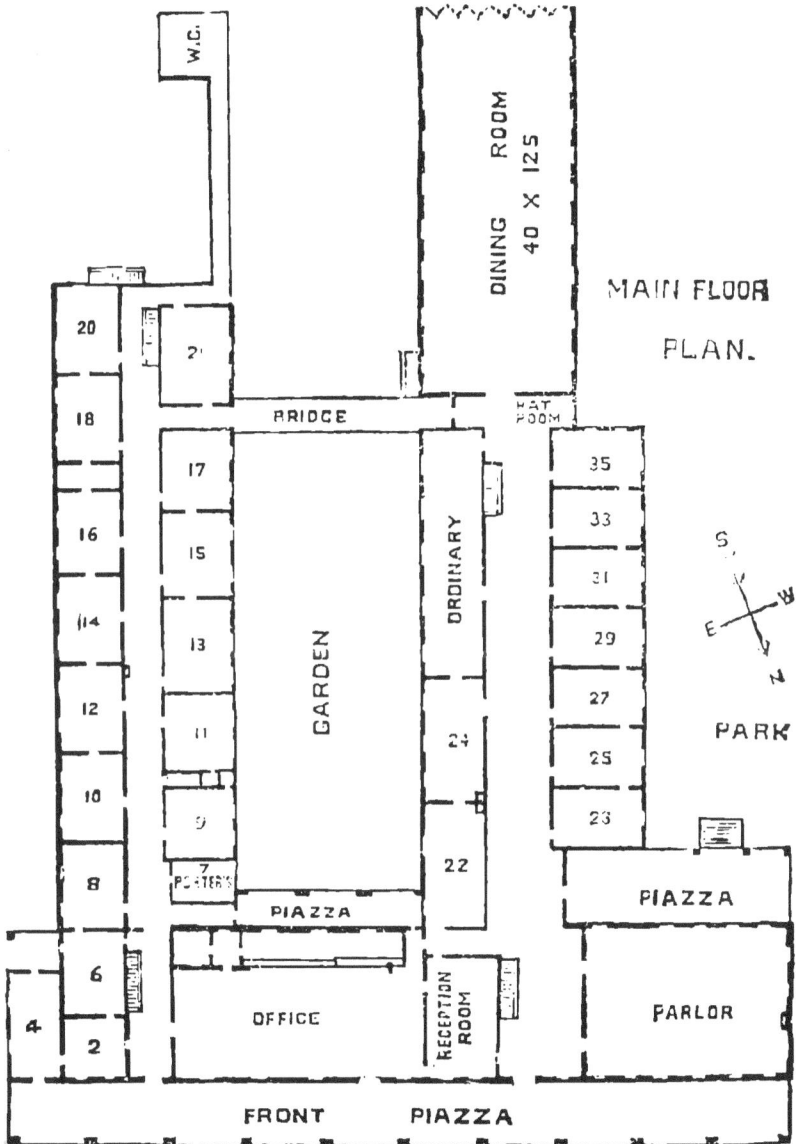

W.C.

DINING ROOM 40 X 125

MAIN FLOOR

PLAN.

BRIDGE

HAT ROOM

20

2

18

17

35

33

16

15

31

ORDINARY

29

14

13

GARDEN

27

12

11

25

24

10

9

23

8

7
PORTERS

22

S

W

E

N

PARK

PIAZZA

PIAZZA

6

RECEPTION ROOM

4

OFFICE

PARLOR

2

FRONT   PIAZZA

FRONTAGE, 175 FEET.   EXTREME DEPTH OF HOTEL, 250 FEET.
ACCOMMODATIONS FOR 500 GUESTS.

The situation is such that all the rooms are open to light, sun and air, and have a pleasant outlook on the grounds and park. The working departments are entirely removed from the main body of the hotel.

THE NEW AMERICAN.

SECOND FLOOR PLAN.

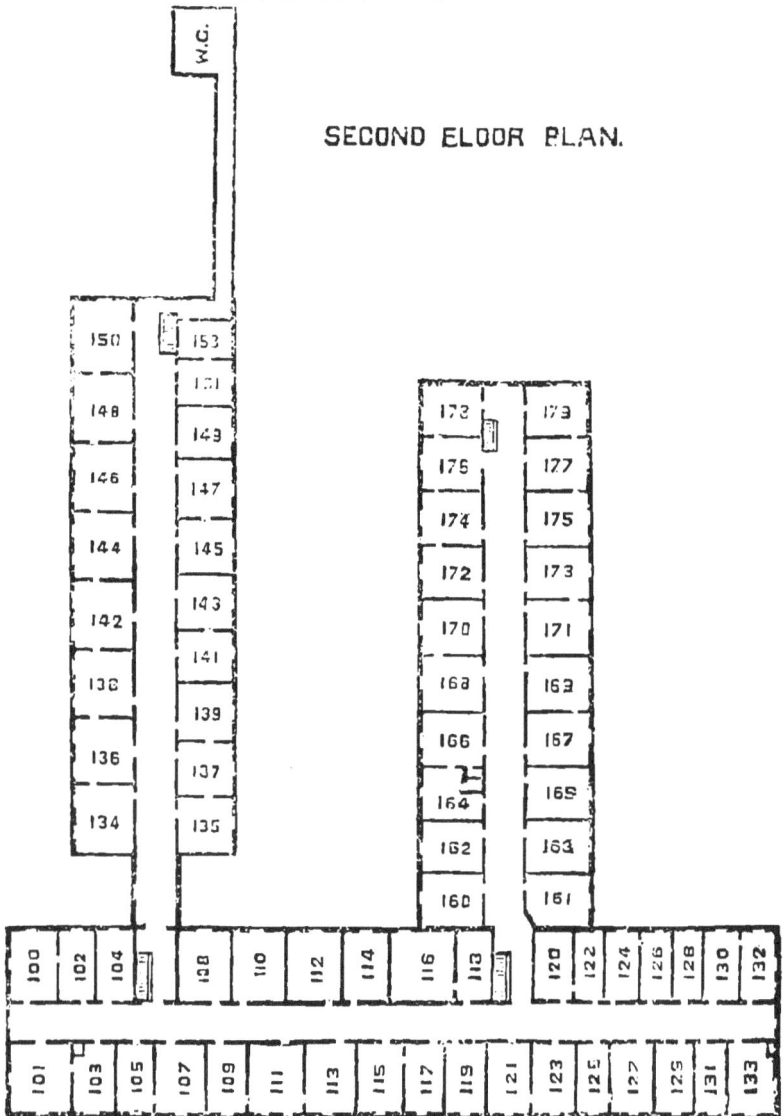

THE NEW AMERICAN.

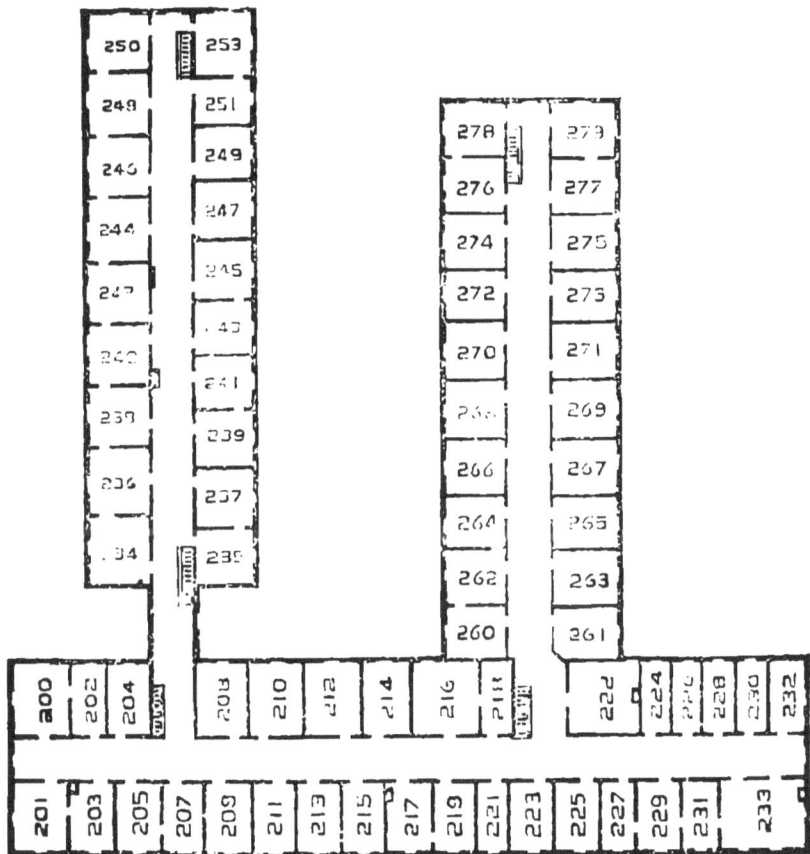

THIRD FLOOR PLAN

SULPHUR SPRING AT THE NEW AMERICAN.
Among the attractions at the *New American* is a spouting spring of
beautiful sulphur water rising eight feet above the surface of the ground.

DRIVES AND OBJECTS OF PLEASURE.

The drives in and about Richfield Springs are many and charming: chief in point of attractiveness is the twelve-mile drive around Canadarago Lake, on which the village is located.

CANADARAGO LAKE.

Canadarago Lake, widely known for the Indian tales associated with it, lies one mile from the center of the village, and is five miles long by two miles broad. It is one of those limpid sheets of which Central New York has so many, and has been pronounced by Continental travelers to be without a rival outside of Italy. It is set in mountains like a gem, and a beautiful island, nine acres in extent, breaks its surface and adds to the loveliness of the view.

At the shore of Canadarago Lake are pleasant groves, with boats and fishing-tackle, croquet and archery grounds, bowling-alleys, a shooting-gallery, etc.

On thy fair bosom, silver lake,
  O I could ever sweep the oar,—
When early birds at morning wake,
  And evening tells us toil is o'er.
      JAMES GATES PERCIVAL.

LAKEVIEW.

Lakeview, at the lower part of the lake, affords a very attractive view.

OTSEGO LAKE, which is reached by an enjoyable drive of six miles, is renowned as the "Glimmerglass" of Cooper's "Deerslayer," on account of the wonderful mirror-like beauty and clearness of the water. A line of stages, including a six-horse "Tally-ho" coach, leaves the Springs three times daily, connecting at the head of the lake with the steamer "Natty Bumppo" for Five-Mile Point, Three-Mile Point, and Cooperstown.

THE VAN HORNESVILLE CAVES AND WATERFALLS.

Ten miles distant from Richfield Springs are objects of surpassing beauty. The formation of the rocks is very remarkable, while the rush of water through this romantic glen makes it a most pleasant resort.

Richfield Springs, N. Y.

FROM THE SONG OF "HIAWATHA."

With him dwelt his dark-eyed daughter,
Wayward as the Minnehaha,
With her moods of shade and sunshine,
Eyes that smiled and frowned alternate
Feet as rapid as the river,
Tresses flowing like the water,
And as musical a laughter;
And he named her from the river,
From the waterfall he named her,
Minnehaha, Laughing Water.

LONGFELLOW.

" O my belovèd rocks that rise
   To awe the earth and brave the skies,
      From some aspiring mountain's crown
   How dearly do I love,
      Giddy with pleasure, to look down,
   And, from the vales, to view the noble heights above!"

WAIONTHA MOUNTAIN is two miles east of Richfield Springs, on its summit is an Observatory seventy feet high, affording a magnificent view of the surrounding country. The range of vision is more than one hundred miles in extent, including part of the Adirondack region, and Otsego.

PANTHER MOUNTAIN, one mile to the south-east, and named for a great Mohican hunter, is as densely covered with forest as in the days of the red man.

MOHICAN HILL, THE HOG BACK, RUM HILL, PROSPECT HILL on the outskirts of the village, THE KYLE, with its subterranean streams, and the remarkable subterranean caverns, known as Kenyon's Cave, are among other points of interest within easy reach.

> Be full, ye courts: be great who will;
> Search for Peace with all your skill;
> Open wide the lofty door,
> Seek her on the marble floor.
> In vain you search; she is not there!
> In vain you search the domes of Care!
> Grass and flowers Quiet treads,
> On the meads and mountain-heads,
> Along with Pleasure, close allied,
> Ever by each other's side.
>   JOHN DYER.

PHYSICIANS.

ALL prominent physicians are now familiar with the wonderful **effects** of Richfield climate and its sulphur waters, and are respectfully referred to.

The resident physicians of Richfield Springs are DRS. NORMAN GETMAN, WM. B. CRAIN, and ALFRED C. CRAIN.

[From *The Gazette*, Washington, D. C.]

ART STUDIES AND OTHER NOTES.

———

STUDYING art by contrast is one of the best ways to judge of the quality of the work, if one is not color-blind, art-blind, and blinded by prejudice.

*   *   *   *   *   *   *   *   *

The "New American," at Richfield Springs, now owned by Uriah Welch, proprietor also of the St. Nicholas Hotel, New York, offers another proof of the advance in artistic ideas. Mr. Welch expended more than $50,000 last year on his hotel at Richfield Springs. It is large and handsomely furnished, the gentlemen's reception room being especially attractive. Stuffed birds of every description, and other game found in the country about Richfield, makes this room a study in natural history. The main hall and parlors, during the early evenings of September, with their open hearths and sparkling fires, the old fashioned crane, the steaming tea kettle, the log beside the mantels, very handsome ones, "grandmother's wheel" and the odd, picturesque chairs which all the grand dames contemplated with longing eyes, and the latest accessories of modern ease and elegance, blended harmoniously. The garden and court were another pleasant feature. Mr. Welch will make many improvements at Richfield for another season. The St. Nicholas, of New York, under Mr. Welch's personal supervision, is one of the best hotels in the land. I am reminded of a bit of history concerning Richfield.

Dr. W. T. Bailey, in his book, "Richfield Springs and Vicinity," gives an interesting sketch of George Robert Twelve Hewes, who was born in the city of Boston, November 5th, 1731. Mr. Lossing, in his history of the Revolution, gives a long account of Mr. Hewes, who was foremost in the destruction of the tea at Boston. This gentleman, with several others disguised as Indians, boarded the several ships and worked so vigorously that within the space of three hours three hundred and forty-two chests of tea were broken up and their contents thrown into the dock. When the Americans invested the city of Boston and many patriots were shut up under the vigilant eyes of the British officers, Hewes was among them. G. R. T. Hewes, Jr., settled at Richfield, and the hero of this sketch died there, at the home of his son, November 5th, 1840, aged one hundred and nine years and two months. I visited the old graveyard, and saw his tombstone, as also that of his wife who lived to a good old age.   B. B.

STEAMER NATTY BUMPPO AND STAGE COACHES.

[From the *Cincinnati Gazette.*]

RICHFIELD SPRINGS, N. Y.

—

RICHFIELD SPRINGS, N. Y., June 25.—Upon the side of a hill among an ocean of hills, at an elevation of over 1,700 feet above the level of the sea, the tourist in search of health or quiet recreation will find the charming village of Richfield Springs surrounded by the most fascinating scenery the imagination can conceive. The principal claim of this truly rural resort is the balminess of its air and general salubrity of its climate, but from a medicinal point of view it also boasts of the most curative sulphur spa in America.

The railroad that brings the visitor to Richfield Springs halts at the depot and goes no further—as much as to say: "You remain here; this is the place you are looking for;" and, truly, if the object of the traveler is to enjoy rest, to enjoy lovely rambles, charming drives, excellent boating and good fishing, together with good living and the most select society, then, indeed, he need go no further. Richfield Springs is one of the quietest places in creation, and it would not suit the tastes of a fast man or a fast woman—we mean those people who desire ostentation and live for it. But that portion of the community who seek in vain for a summer resort where all is comfort and repose, having once found Richfield Springs will never forget to visit it annually when health or disposition demand thorough restfulness. Hence it is that of the 3,000 or so visitors that come here nearly all are annual visitors, and, strange to say, they come from almost every State in the Union, and even from the remotest Territories. Why, then, one may ask, are there not more people at Richfield Springs? That is a question that is often asked, but may be answered very readily by saying the people who now come here are not anxious that the place shall be crowded. They have a good thing, and, to use a very expressive slang phrase, they do not wish to "give it away." In other words, they do not desire to make the place common, hence they never invite any but their very best and warmest friends to visit Richfield Springs, and true it is that if the people of large cities knew of half the real attractions of this place it would soon lose one of the main attractions it now boasts of, and that is its rare real, unartificial life.

A couple of streets of quiet, rustic, lovely cottages, two large hotels, a few small hotels or boarding houses, and eight or ten country stores, and Richfield Springs is enumerated, all save the four or five churches and the numerous feathered tribes, and these latter are quite innumerable. Probably there is no village in America known as a resort that could give such an enormous census of birds, and they include every species of song bird known in the Northern and Eastern States. Along the line of the main street, which is more like a beautiful road leading through a park than a street, the robins have nests in every tree, and as every house, even the humblest, has a garden or lawn, either in the front or rear, the robins can be counted in them in scores, and so tame are they that one can almost handle them. A more delightful spot for children could hardly be found on earth. From the village streets wherever the eye wanders it goes up, up to some lofty hill fantastically crowned with trees of a greenness as beautiful as the emerald, and these again rest against a sky of such pure amethystic blue as forms at all times a picture refreshing to the mind and invigorating to the senses. The breezes from the myriads of hills come hither and thither, never, even on the hottest day of summer, being absent, but in zephyrs swaying the tops of the tall trees that line every street and avenue within and around the village for miles.

Of the curative waters and baths, it may be remarked that all leading physicians throughout the country are familiar with their properties and can inform the reader better of their usefulness than we can, but of the pure salubrious air no words can exaggerate its importance, and it is as much a peculiarity of this locality as it is of Montpelier in France, on the shores of the Mediterranean, a place renowned for ages for its pure air and mild climate.

Within a mile, along a most romantic walk, is the charming Lake Canadarago. It is five miles long, and varies from one to two miles in width. A small hotel, the "Lake House," stands on its margin, and here boats and bait for fishing can be hired for a small price. As lovely a sheet of water as Switzerland or any country under the sun can boast, is Cana-

darago.   At a distance of six miles, over the mountains, is situated
Lake Otsego, immortalized by Cooper, and on its delightful border is
Cooperstown, named in honor of the novelist.   Omnibuses and four-
horse stages run to the lake, and small steamers ply on it.   Cooperstown itself looks the very picture of a Swiss hamlet, surrounded, as it
is, by scenes of peerless beauty.   The widely diversified panoramas of
mountain, hillside, lake, and valley within the environments of what
may be called the surroundings of Richfield Springs, presents irresisti-
ble fascinations to the mere tourist, the invalid, or sportsman who is a
Walton, for these surrounding lakes abound in perch, bass, pickerel, etc.
The drives are almost innumerable, and through a country smiling with
plenty.   The hop-poles, with their vines, of which there are acres scat-
tered here and there, diversify the landscape and remind one of Kent,
England.   From an observatory near by the eye can survey the country
for fifty miles, including six different lakes.   The Hog Back is a pecul-
iar hill of great height, affording views of extraordinary beauty.   In its
immediate locality is a great natural wonder called by the natives "The
Kyle," a great natural basin, into which flows a mountain stream of
considerable volume and then disappears through a number of openings
into the ground and goes—no man has ever found out where !   No
railroad whistles or bell ringing at all hours of the day at Richfield
Springs !   No omnibuses rattle over streets !   No sounds of city life.
All is absolute quiet save occasionally the clear ringing sound of the
village blacksmith's hammer, the robin's morning and evening song, or

" THE BEES' DREAMY CHIME."

And yet there is life and enough to satisfy an ordinary mortal in a
a quiet way.   The Spring Park shows throngs of gaily dressed ladies
promenading, or on rustic seats plying their needles or reading.   The
well ordered carriages pass through the village street, either going to or
returning from the drive, and when the train from New York is due in

the evening, the village actually wakes up for half an hour, and at one view shows its entire population. But by eight o'clock all is again still, almost as Spring Grove Cemetery, except on hop nights, when alternately at the Spring House or American Hotel, on certain evenings during the week, those who care to indulge in the dancing, to music that is not all a noise, but to the best that New York City can furnish in string bands, can amuse themselves to the heart's content. But even the nights of revelry at Richfield Springs are subdued and quiet, and moderation guides every step, and hence those who sojourn here leave it with that inestimable boon that King Solomon said was the greatest possession that man could have good health.

The principal hotel of Richfield Springs is the New American, owned by the well-known Uriah Welch, Esq., proprietor of the St. Nicholas Hotel, of New York, accommodating about five hundred guests. The New American is directly opposite the park and the celebrated sulphur springs. The American is a modern hotel in every sense of the word, and not being the rendezvous of a miscellaneous crowd, as large hotels are at common resorts, it is rather an elegant home than a hotel. Here spaciousness seems to have been the main aim, and this is carried out in everything piazzas, parlors, halls, dining-rooms, everywhere. Some of those persons who live in little rooms at so called fashionable watering places, which are so small that a cat could not be gently swung around by the tail, would open their eyes in wonder at the size of the sleeping rooms in this house, and such ample furniture, too, and such air in every department ! Three-fourths of the people who live in hotels have no idea of how the other fourth, who are thoroughly posted, live. It is only by traveling about one finds the thing out. It is safe to say that the rooms in the New American are double, and in many cases triple, the size of those ordinarily to be found in summer hotels.

But this is also a winter hotel as well as a summer one, and this is a provision that is an innovation in its way. Everybody knows that under our variable climate we sometimes have in the height of summer a couple of cold, damp, wet days with all the horrors of midwinter. At such a time the New American in half an hour puts on a new phase, and lo: the parlors are made bright by the ruddy glow of huge logs ablaze in the great open, old fashioned fireplaces, like unto those of the olden time, and besides, the dining-room is heated by steam. With these contrivances, if a bad day comes, life indoors is made cozy and comfortable. All through this great house one walks on the softest and richest of carpets Even the office is carpeted to the street door, or rather avenue, for avenue it is. The bar is carpeted, every floor everywhere is carpeted. The walls are hung with interesting pictures of real merit, and, as before stated, the hotel is more like a home than a house of public entertainment. One of the greatest drawbacks to most country resorts is the fact that most of the hotels, even where they are first-class in all the appointments, are behind the best city hotels in the matter of cuisine. This is the point upon which the New American stands out in bold relief. Here is a bill of fare for you every day that might tickle the palate of an Archbishop, or even a Grand Duke: Fresh fish from the lakes, many varieties; fresh vegetables from the garden, milk and cream direct from the dairy, fresh young chickens that crow in the morning of the day they appear on the bill of fare, with all the etceteras that the New York markets furnish, cooked by chefs from the St. Nicholas.

There are several ways of reaching Richfield Springs, but the most direct from New York City is via the 10:30 A.M. express, N. Y. C. & H. R. Railroad, drawing-room cars through without change, arriving at 7:30 P.M. Cincinnatians can intercept this train at Utica. Other routes from the East are by the Albany and Troy boats and the rail above mentioned, or Delaware & Hudson Company's Susquehanna Division to Cooperstown, connecting with the Otsego Lake boats and stages, arriving at 7 P.M.; also, by the Delaware, Lackawanna & Western Railroad 8 A.M. train, via Delaware, Water Gap, Scranton, and Binghamton, arriving at 9 P.M.

There are stages and private conveyances to be had at Herkimer, on the N. Y. C. Road on arrival of all trains, affording a most delightful twelve-mile drive over the hills through scenery unsurpassed in the State.

VISITORS.

—

THE many patrons of the New American can be referred to, as to the standard of the House and its select company.

We have only room in this pamphlet for a few of the prominent names from New York City of those who have been its guests during the present management:

Aymar, Mrs. S.
Aymar, Miss.
Aymar, Mr. Wm.
Acker, Mr. Chas. L. and wife.
Allen, Mr. Edwin and wife.
Alexander, Mr. Jno. F.
Adsit, Mrs. Fannie E.
Abernethey, Mrs. Chas.
Allen, Dr. and Mrs. J.
Adams, Mr. and Mrs. Sam'l R.
Bates, Mr. E. C. and wife.
Bell, Mrs. Wm.
Blackford, Mr. E. G. and family.
Brown, Mr. O. M. and wife.
Beardslee, Mrs. Paul.
Banker, Mrs. and Miss.
Benkard, Mr. J. and family.
Brown, Mr. and Mrs. Lewis B.
Boynton, Dr. F. H.
Blauvelt, Mr. J. H.
Buckley, Dr. L. D.
Brush, Mrs. and Miss.
Brush, Mr. Louis S.

Borse, Mrs. Thos. and daughter.
Barnard, President and Mrs. F. A.
Baiz, Mr. Jacob and family.
Barrios, President and family.
Clinton, Hon. Henry L. and wife.
Cotting, Mr. A. and family.
Coleman, Mr. Jas. H. and family.
Currier, Mr. and Mrs. F. H.
Chamberlin, Mr. J. and family.
Culver, Mrs. A. R. and family.
Chase, Mr. S. G. and wife.
Cranston, Mr. Henry.
Clarkson, Mrs. L. A.
Chardavoyne, Mr. G. M.
Colfax, Mr. E. A. and family.
Coggeshall, Mr. and Mrs. E. I.
Cooke, Mr. and Mrs. W. H.
Chapman, Mrs. C. B.
Davis, Mr. J. W. and family.
Delgado, Mr. J. M. and wife.
Dayton, Miss Etta.
Davis, Mrs. F. M.
Dorr, Mrs. A. I.

Dorr, Mrs. Maxwell.
Deems, Rev. Dr. Chas.
Donnells, Mr. Nath. and wife.
Douglas, Mr. Jno. A. and family.
Ditson, Mr. Charles H.
DeLussan, Mrs. P.
DeLussan, Miss Zalie.
Eno, Mr. Amos R. and family.
Everson, Mr. D. S. and wife.
Elsworth, Miss S. A.
Embury, Mrs. A. B. and daughters.
Edson, Misses.
Enriquez, Col. M.
Fisher, Mr. E. A. and family.
Farrington, Mr. E. A. and wife.
Faulkner, Mr. E. H. and wife.
Fanshawe, Mr. H. A. and family.
Fisher, Mr. J. H. and family.
Faye, Mr. Thos. and family.
Fonda, Mr. Thos. and family
Farnum, Mr. W. H. and wife.
Fisher, Mr. E. A. and family.
Gilbert, Dr. J. B.
Godfrey, C. H. and family.
Grannis, Mr. J. F. and wife.
Graham, Miss.
Gibbs, Mr. and Mrs. Theo. K.
Gautier, Mrs. J. H. and family
Garrison, Mrs.
Gesner, Mrs. and Miss.
Gillespie, Mr. L. C. and family.
Haight, Mr. E. C. and wife.
Hartshorn, Mr. A. B. and wife.
Harnett, Mr. Richard V.
Hicks, Dr. and family.
Hart, Mr. W. H. and wife.
Houghton, Mr. F. R. and wife.

Hitchings, Mrs. C. T. and family.
Haight, Mr. H. J. and wife.
Hale, Mr. James and family.
Haight, Miss A. B.
Hunter, Mrs. J. F.
Hall, Mr. and Mrs. R. L.
Hearn, Mr. Geo. A., Jr., and family.
Hollins, Mr. H. B. and family.
Halsey, Gen'l Robt. and family.
Harris, Mrs. Edward.
Haggin, Mr. B. A. and family.
Hungerford, Mrs.
Hoagland, Mrs. S. A. and family.
Helm, Mrs. C. A.
Hinkley, Mr. Chas.
Jones, Col. Floyd.
Jones, Miss S. Floyd.
Johnson, Mr. Bradish, Jr., and family.
Kirkham, Mr. H. P. and family.
Knapp, Mrs. A. E.
Knapp, Mr. W. Percy.
Kingsland, Mr. A. A.
Kellogg, Mr. A. N. and family.
LeBoutellier, Mr. George.
Little, Mr. E. and family.
Lord, Miss.
Lord, Mr. and Mrs. D. D.
Lorillard, Mrs. Pierre and family.
Lent, Miss Alice.
Lent, Mr. Wm. B.
Livingston, Mrs. L.
Livingston, Mr. P. L.
Musgrave, Mr. S. B. and family.
Martinez, Mr. Alex. and family.
McAlpin, Mrs. Ch.
Marsh, Mr. A. and family.
Morris, Mr. C. O. and family.

McLean, Mr. Geo. H. and family.
Marshall, Mrs. J. R.
Muller, Mr. A. H. and family.
Mygatt, Mr. W. R. and wife.
McLean, Misses E. and M.
Mortimer, Mr. and Mrs. J. H.
Millan, Miss F.
Mauriac, Mr. and Mrs. E. A.
Mesier, Mr. L.
Meeker, Mr. C. B. and family.
Nevins, Mr. R. L. and family.
Nott, Dr. F. J.
Ormiston, Rev. Dr. and wife.
O'Donohue, Mr. T. J.
Obrig, Mr. A. and wife.
Olcott, Mrs. and Miss.
Prentice, Mrs. Wm. P. and family.
Pearsall, Mr. Thos. E. and family.
Pardee, Mrs.
Peck, Mr. Charles M. and family.
Rapallo, Mr. E. T.
Robbins, Mr. Amos.
Robbins, Mr. A. S. and family.
Razee, Mrs. S. W.
Rathburn, Mr. O. J.
Remsen, Miss Lizzie.
Rayner, Mr. and Mrs. J. A.
Robbins, Mr. G. A. and family.
Roberts, Mr. Chas., Jr.
Roberts, Mr. and Mrs. J. K.
Robinson, Miss May.
Robinson, Miss Bertha.
Redmond, Mr. W.
Reyburn, Mr. and Mrs. W. S.
Sloane, Mr. Geo. H. and wife.
Shephard, Mr. Elliott F. and wife.
Squires, Mr. G. H. and wife.

Sands, Mr. D. C. and wife.
Stedman, Mr. E. C. and family.
Schermerhorn, Mr. Chas. and wife.
Sherman, Mr. B. B. and wife.
Sloane, Mrs. Geo.
Sloane, Miss.
Stedman, Mr. Arthur G.
Sillcocks, Mr. W. S. and family.
Seabury, Mrs. H.
Schmidt, Mr. and Mrs. Wm.
Spencer, Mrs. Oscar H.
Smith, Mr. Charles H. and family.
Stevens, Mr. Jno. R. and family.
Smith, Mr. J. B. and family.
Stoddard, Mr. and Mrs. R. H.
Smith, Mr. Ed. F.
Townsend, Mr. R. H. L. and wife.
Tappan, Mrs. J. U. and daughter.
Thorn, Mr. G. A. and family.
Townsend, Mr. Geo. Alfred and wife.
Todd, Mr. Robt. F. and wife.
Thompson, Mr. C. A. and family.
Travers, Mrs. and Miss.
Travers, Mrs. Gilbert and family.
Thompson, Mrs. A. E.
Townsend, Mrs. Isaac.
Townsend, Miss.
Utley, Mrs. H.
Van Buren, Mr. Jno. D.
Van Nest, Mrs. and Miss.
Vanderbilt, Mrs. W. H. and family.
Van Volkenburgh, Mr. and Mrs. P.
Vanderbilt, Mr. J. H., Jr., and family.
Vanderbilt, Mr. John.
Vanderbilt, Miss.
Vanderhoef, Mr. G. W.
Work, Mr. Frank.

Work, Miss.
Wharton, Mr. W. F. and family.
Wing, Mr. Chas. T. and family.
Whitney, Mr. D. J. and wife.
Wilson, Mr. Jno. D. and wife.
Wysong, Mr. Jno. J. and wife.
Wall, Mrs. Chas. and family.
Watson, Mr. Jno. H. and family.
White, Dr. T. H.
Wilson, Mrs. C. H.

Work, Mr. George.
Wood, Mr. and Mrs. T. H.
Wetherell, Mr. and Mrs. N.
Work, Mr. and Mrs. Jno. C.
Whitman, Mr. N.
Warren, Mr. and Mrs. Ira D.
Wright, Mr. J. Hood and family.
White, Mr. and Mrs. S. Nelson.
Williams, Mr. Jno. L. and family.
Williams, Mrs. and Miss.

A Summer School

OF THE

AMERICAN + INSTITUTE + OF + CHRISTIAN + PHILOSOPHY

Will be held at Richfield Springs, beginning on Tuesday, August 21st, and closing on Thursday, August 30th, 1883. Popular Lectures will be delivered on TIMELY TOPICS of Philosophy and Religion, together with discussions of the themes, in which many learned and genial gentlemen will participate. Lectures have already been engaged from

Prest. DARLING, of Hamilton College.

Rev. Dr. DEEMS, of New York,

Rev. Dr. ERRET, of Cincinnati,

Rev. Dr. FRANCIS L. PATTON, of Princeton,

Prest. PORTER, of Yale College,

Prest. POTTER, of Union College,

Rev. Dr. RYLANCE, of New York,

Prof. WELCH, of Auburn,

and Prest. WHITE, of Cornell.

Rev. Dr. JOSEPH PARKER, of London, is expected.

Others may be Secured.

It will be a delightful reunion of cultivated and celebrated men brought together by the American Institute of Christian Philosophy. A special programme will be announced before the assembling of the School.

Those who desire information in regard to the American Institute of Christian Philosophy, may address its President, Charles F. Deems, D.D., LL.D., Pastor of the Church of the Strangers, New York.

RICHFIELD SPRINGS.

Dr. W. B. Crain,

MAIN STREET,

RICHFIELD SPRINGS.

Dr. ALFRED CRAIN,

LAKE STREET,

Richfield Springs.

Dr. N. GETMAN,

MAIN STREET,

OFFICE HOURS: { 9 to 11 A. M.
7 to 9 P. M. }

RICHFIELD SPA, N. Y.

Geo. R. Smith,

Professor of MASSAGE,

During July and August at - - Richfield Springs.
Balance of the Year at - Windsor Hotel, New York.

FIRST NATIONAL BANK, Richfield Springs, N. Y.

NORMAN GETMAN, Pres., MYRON A McKEE, Cashier,
TRANSACTS A GENERAL BANKING BUSINESS.

Buy and sell Foreign Exchanges. Collections promptly remitted for at lowest rates.
New York Correspondent, MERCANTILE NATIONAL BANK.
Albany, NATIONAL ALBANY EXCHANGE BANK.

HOTELS.

Among the very few strictly first-class Hotels in New York may be mentioned the following, which are especially noted for elegance, as well as for that particular attention which contributes so much to comfort.

ALBEMARLE HOTEL,

EUROPEAN PLAN,

MADISON SQUARE & TWENTY-FOURTH STREET.

FIFTH AVENUE HOTEL,

American Plan.   MADISON SQUARE.

GRAND HOTEL,

EUROPEAN PLAN,

BROADWAY, CORNER THIRTY-FIRST STREET.

UTICA, N. Y.

Tourists for Richfield Springs, Trenton Falls, Thousand Islands, and Niagara Falls, will find BAGG'S HOTEL and the BUTTERFIELD HOUSE, Utica, comfortable resting-places. Bagg's Hotel Farm, East Utica, a model hotel farm, supplies these hotels with pure milk and cream from its celebrated Alderney herd, fresh vegetables, poultry, eggs, and creamery butter; has for sale the very best Berkshire and small Yorkshire pigs, light Brahma fowls, and Alderney cows.

T. R. PROCTOR, Proprietor.

The business houses herein mentioned have an exceptional reputation
for fair dealing, and can be fully relied upon by parties
out of the city who may desire to send
them orders.

ACKER, MERRALL & CONDIT,

EUGENE G. BLACKFORD,

FISH,

FULTON MARKET.

A. & E. ROBBINS,
Poultry and Game,
FULTON MARKET.

MIDDLETON, CARMAN & CO.,
FISH,
Fulton Market.

KNAPP & VAN NOSTRAND,
POULTRY,
WASHINGTON MARKET.

GEO. B. WEAVER.
Fish,
WASHINGTON MARKET.

JAMES McCALL,
Country Produce and Fruits,   378 Greenwich Street.

E. J. LARRABEE & CO.,
Fine Biscuit,   ALBANY, AND 143 CHAMBERS STREET, N. Y.

J. D. KINNER, PROVISION DEALER,
52 & 54 CENTRE MARKET.   Country Pork, Sausages, and Excelsior Hams a specialty.

E. B. DOUGLASS & SON
Maple Avenue Farm, Shoreham, Vt.   Finest Jersey Butter. Supplying New American and St. Nicholas.

St. Nicholas Hotel

BROADWAY,

NEW YORK,

URIAH WELCH, - Proprietor.

AN HISTORIC BIRD.

The Cock is an important bird. He is historical. A cock assured Themistocles of his victory over Xerxes. Aristophanes tells us that he reigned supreme over Persia before the time of Darius and Megabazus. Numa Pompilius was inspired by a cock, and Romulus was influenced by the same bird in his decision as to the site of Rome. He was sacred to Mars, Apollo, Mercury and Æsculapius. Mohammed found a cock in the first heaven, so huge a bird that his crest touched the second heaven. The Moslem doctors say that Allah lends a willing ear to him who reads the Koran, to him who prays for pardon, and to the cock, whose chant is divine melody. When this cock ceases to crow the day of judgment will be at hand. The cock on church spires is to remind men not to deny their Lord as Peter did. Peter le Neve says that the cock was the warlike ensign of the Goths, as it is to the present day of the Malays, and that therefore it was put in Gothic churches for ornament. When placed on hotels, as is customary in some parts of Switzerland and France, especially Normandy, and as is the case in one notable instance in New York, it is the emblem signifying " Good cheer within."—*London Graphic.*

ROUTE ✤ FOR ✤ HORSES ✤ AND ÷ CARRIAGES,

OTHERWISE THAN SHIPMENT BY RAIL.

BOAT TO ALBANY, thence by the Great-Western Turnpike

GASKINS,	16	miles.
ESPERANCE,	32	"
SLOANE VILLAGE,	36	"
CARLISLE, .	40	"
SHARON SPRINGS,	44	"
ROCKVILLE,	48	"
CHERRY VALLEY,	52	"
SPRINGFIELD CORNERS,	57	
WEST SPRINGFIELD,	59	"
LITTLE LAKES,	63	"
RICHFIELD SPRINGS,	66	"

Good Stable Accommodations at ESPERANCE, SHARON SPRINGS and CHERRY VALLEY.

www.ingramcontent.com/pod-product-compliance
Lightning Source LLC
Chambersburg PA
CBHW031822090426

42739CB00008B/1374